JOHANN SEBASTIAN BACH

MAGNIFICAT

für SSATB soli, Chor und Orchester
for SSATB Soli, Choir and Orchestra

D-Dur / D major
BWV 243

Mit vier weihnachtlichen Einlagesätzen
aus der ersten Fassung in Es-Dur (BWV 243a)

With Four Additional Christmas Hymns
from the First Version in E-flat major (BWV 243a)

Herausgegeben von / Edited by

Hans-Joachim Schulze

Klavierauszug von / Vocal Score by

Johannes Muntschick

ALLE RECHTE VORBEHALTEN · ALL RIGHTS RESERVED

EDITION PETERS

Leipzig · London · New York

INHALT / CONTENTS

1. Magnificat (Coro) 1
2. Et exsultavit (Soprano II solo) 11
3. Quia respexit (Soprano I solo) 16
4. Omnes generationes (Coro) 19
5. Quia fecit mihi magna (Basso solo) 26
6. Et misericordia (Alto solo, Tenore solo) 29
7. Fecit potentiam (Coro) 34
8. Deposuit (Tenore solo) 42
9. Esurientes (Alto solo) 47
10. Suscepit Israel (Soprano I solo, Soprano II solo, Alto solo) 52
11. Sicut locutus est (Coro) 56
12. Gloria Patri (Coro) 63

Vier weihnachtliche Einlagesätze aus der ersten Fassung in Es-Dur (BWV 243a)
Four Additional Christmas Hymns from the First Version in E-flat major (BWV 243a)

A. Vom Himmel hoch (Coro), nach Nr. 2 72
B. Freut euch und jubiliert (Coro), nach Nr. 5 75
C. Gloria in excelsis (Coro), nach Nr. 7 78
D. Virga Jesse floruit (Soprano solo, Basso solo), nach Nr. 9 81

NACHWORT 86
CONCLUDING REMARKS 88

BESETZUNG / ORCHESTRATION

Tromba I/II/III in D – Timpani in D/A
Flauto traverso I/II – Oboe I/II (anche Oboe d'amore I/II)
Violino I/II – Viola
Organo – Continuo: Violoncello – Violone – Fagotto
Soli e Coro: Soprano I/II – Alto – Tenore – Basso

Aufführungsdauer / Duration: ca. 45 Min.

MAGNIFICAT

1. Magnificat

J. S. Bach (1685-1750)
BWV 243
Herausgegeben von H. J. Schulze
Klavierauszug von J. Muntschick

2. Et exsultavit

A. Vom Himmel hoch da komm ich her

(Beiheft S. 2 – Supplement p. 2)

3. Quia respexit

4. Omnes generationes

5. Quia fecit mihi magna

B. Freut euch und jubiliert

(Beiheft S. 5 – Supplement p. 5)

6. Et misericordia

7. Fecit potentiam

C. Gloria in excelsis Deo
(Beiheft S. 8 – Supplement p. 8)

8. Deposuit

9. Esurientes

D. Virga Jesse floruit

(Beiheft S. 11 – Supplement p. 11)

10. Suscepit Israel

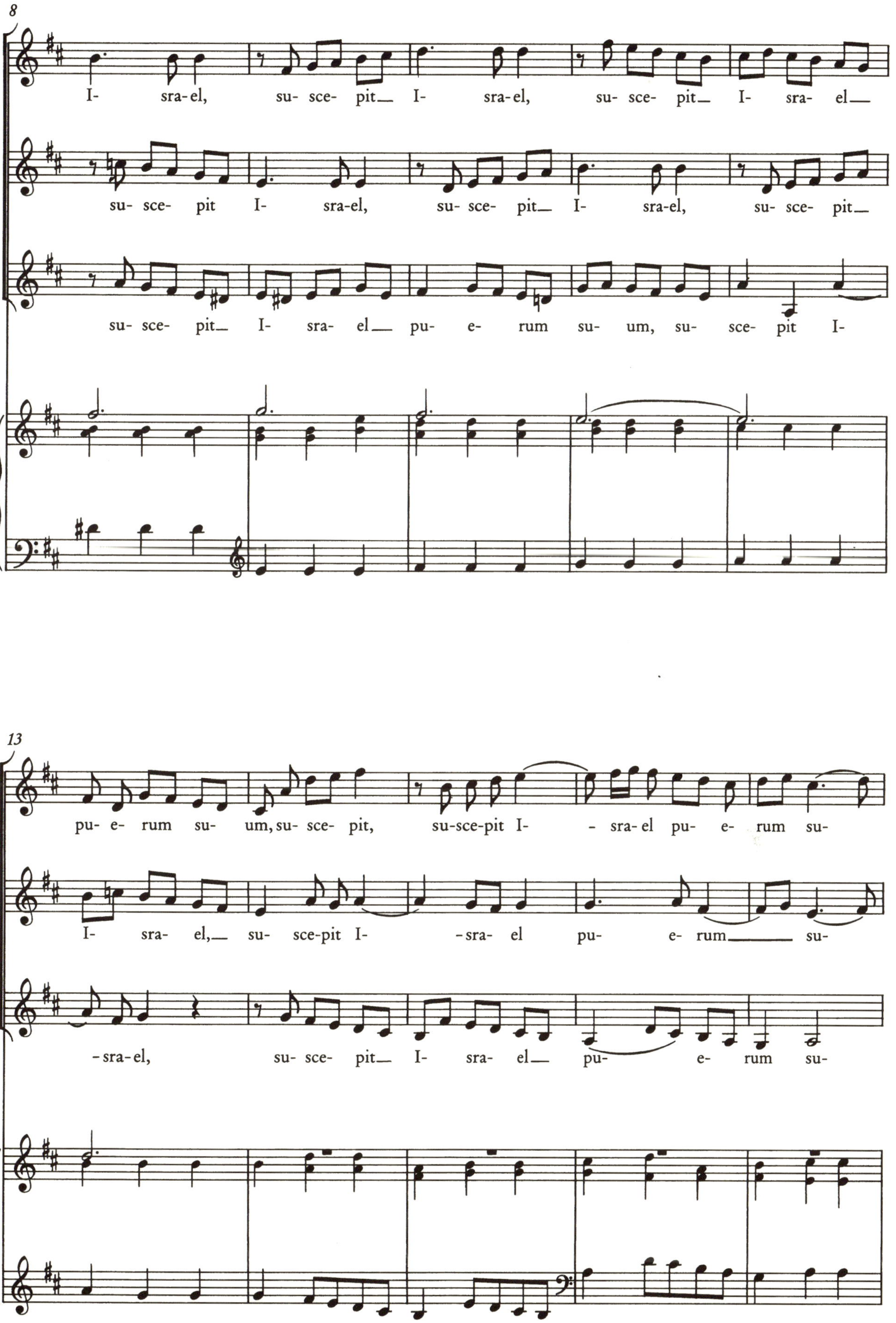
8
I- sra-el, su- sce- pit I- sra-el, su- sce- pit I- sra- el
su- sce- pit I- sra-el, su- sce- pit I- sra-el, su- sce- pit
su- sce- pit I- sra- el pu- e- rum su- um, su- sce- pit I-
13
pu- e- rum su- um, su- sce- pit, su-sce-pit I- - sra- el pu- e- rum su-
I- sra- el, su- sce-pit I- -sra- el pu- e- rum su-
-sra-el, su- sce- pit I- sra- el pu- e- rum su-

11. Sicut locutus est

12. Gloria Patri

Vier weihnachtliche Einlagesätze
aus der ersten Fassung in Es-Dur (BWV 243a)

Four Additional Christmas Hymns
from the First Version in E-flat major (BWV 243a)

A. Vom Himmel hoch

J. S. Bach (1685-1750)

Herausgegeben von H. J. Schulze

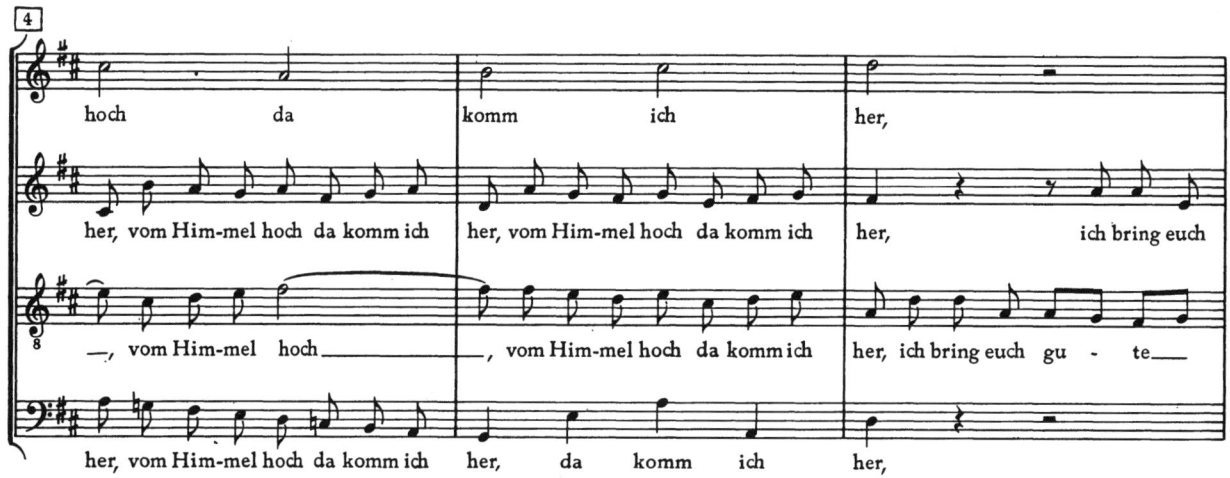

B. Freut euch und jubiliert

C. Gloria in excelsis

D. Virga Jesse floruit

NACHWORT

Als eines der Cantica maiora im Offizium der römischen Kirche nimmt das Magnificat (Lobgesang Mariä, Canticum Beatae Mariae Virginis) seit jeher einen bevorzugten Platz in der Liturgie ein und bildet – nachweisbar seit dem 6. Jahrhundert – den Höhepunkt der Vesper. Neben dem traditionellen psalmodischen Vortrag seines neutestamentlichen Textes (Lukas 1,46–55) trat seit dem Zeitalter der „niederländischen Polyphonie" die motettische Bearbeitung, deren vom 15. Jahrhundert an zu verfolgende reichverzweigte Literatur nahezu alle bedeutenderen Namen von Dunstable und Dufay bis zu Morales, Lasso, Palestrina und Johann Walter mit umfaßt.

Nachgerade unübersehbar sind Zahl und Formenschatz der kunstvollen konzertierenden Ausgestaltung seit Beginn des 17. Jahrhunderts, bei der der Magnificattext mit Requiem und Tedeum etwa gleichauf in der Gunst der Komponisten stand. Stellvertretend für viele seien aus dem 17. Jahrhundert Monteverdi, Schütz und Buxtehude genannt, aus dem 18. Jahrhundert Albinoni, die Bach-Söhne Carl Philipp Emanuel und Johann Christian, Caldara, Galuppi, Graupner, Harrer, W. A. Mozart, Sammartini, Telemann, Vivaldi und Zelenka. Nach einer Talsenke im 19. Jahrhundert – erwähnenswert erscheint allenfalls Felix Mendelssohn-Bartholdy – sind in neuerer Zeit wieder gewichtigere Beiträge zu verzeichnen, so von Ernst Pepping und Krzystof Penderecki.

Als Gipfelwerk in dieser Traditionskette darf ohne Frage Johann Sebastian Bachs Komposition gelten, die an instrumentalem Glanz, Konzentration und Dichte, Vielfalt der Satzcharaktere und Tiefe der Textexegese alle bis dahin gesetzten Maßstäbe übertrifft. Ob das in zwei Fassungen (Es-Dur und D-Dur) überlieferte Werk Bachs einzigen Beitrag zur Gattung Magnificat darstellt, bleibt ungewiß, zumal in Nachlaß des Thomaskantors „viele Oratorien, Messen, Magnificat, einzelne Sanctus..." vorhanden gewesen sein sollen. Ein lange Zeit unerreichbares sogenanntes „Kleines Magnificat" für Sopransolo und Instrumente erwies sich nach seiner Wiederauffindung als etwa 1708 entstandene Kirchenkantate, deren Kompositionsautograph auf Georg Philipp Telemann als Autor zu deuten schien, ohne daß bislang letzte Klarheit darüber zu erreichen gewesen wäre.

In seiner Es-Dur-Fassung (BWV 243a) entstand Bachs Magnificat allem Anschein nach im Dezember 1723 als erstes größeres Vokalwerk nach dem Antritt des Leipziger Thomaskantorats. Während des *tempus clausum*, den nach dem ersten Advent beginnenden und bis zum vierten Advent reichenden musiklosen Wochen, stand zum ersten Male ausreichend Zeit zur Verfügung, um ein Werk dieses Umfanges zu vollenden, das sich in allen Teilen als Originalkomposition erweist. Flüchtiger Duktus und Korrekturreichtum der autographen Partitur sind hier nicht als Symptome etwaiger Zeitbedrängnis anzusehen, sondern deuten im Gegenteil auf eine besonders sorgfältige Ausarbeitung.

Daß für Bach gleichwohl eine Anfangssituation vorlag, läßt sich verschiedenen Indizien entnehmen. Hierzu gehört etwa eine gewisse Unsicherheit hinsichtlich der Chorbesetzung, bei der zunächst nur an vier Singstimmen gedacht war, dann an eine Fünfstimmigkeit mit Sopran, Alt I und II, Tenor und Baß, ehe Bach sich für eine Teilung in Sopran I und II entschied. Die rätselhafte, erst- und einmalige Wahl der Tonart Es-Dur für ein mit Trompeten und Pauken besetztes Werk könnte sich damit erklären, daß Bach von den für das Bläserensemble bisher ausschließlich eingesetzten C-Stimmung abzuweichen beabsichtigte, die nachmals geradezu als Norm geltende D-Stimmung jedoch noch nicht erprobt hatte und einen entsprechenden Versuch erst zu Neujahr 1724 unternahm. Daß Bach von vornherein auf das als Ausweg anderwärts gelegentlich nachweisbare Verfahren einer Darbietung mit Holzbläsern im „tiefen Kammerton" und tiefer gestimmten Streichinstrumenten gezielt habe (Notierung in Es = klingend D), die die Verwendung von D-Trompeten ermöglicht hätte, erscheint demgegenüber weniger glaubhaft. Die nachträgliche, nicht ohne Einbußen für die tonartliche Ausgewogenheit des Werkganzen vollzogene Komposition der vier weihnachtlichen Einlagesätze deutet in gleicher Weise auf Bachs mangelnde Vertrautheit mit gewissen Leipziger Gepflogenheiten. Wenn Bach sich im ersten Amtsjahr die komplizierte Liturgie des Ersten Adventssonntages vorsorglich in eine Kantatenpartitur notierte und sich noch im April 1724 in einer Konfliktsituation als einen *„Fremden"* bezeichnete, *„so hiesiger Gewohnheiten nicht kundig"*, so darf auch hinsichtlich des Es-Dur-Magnificats unbedenklich von einem Stadium des Suchens, Erprobens und Experimentierens gesprochen werden.

Im Vespergottesdienst der Leipziger Hauptkirchen St. Nikolai und St. Thomae wurde *„das Magnificat an gemeinen Sonntagen Teutsch gesungen, an hohen Festen aber Lateinisch musiciret"* (Chr. E. Sicul, *Annales Lipsienses*, Leipzig 1717). „Hohe Feste" im vorgenannten Sinne waren die jeweils ersten beiden Feiertage von Weihnachten, Ostern und Pfingsten; Gelegenheit zur „musikalischen" (konzertierenden) Darbietung des Magnificats gaben offenbar aber auch andere Feiertage wie Himmelfahrt oder die Marienfeste.

Da es üblich war, am ersten Feiertag eines hohen Festes die „Hauptmusik" (Kantate) im Vormittagsgottesdienst der Nikolaikirche aufzuführen und im Vespergottesdienst der Thomaskirche zu wiederholen (am zweiten Feiertag wurde die Reihenfolge umgekehrt), so ist die erste Aufführung des Magnificats in der Es-Dur-Fassung am Nachmittag des 25. Dezember 1723 in der Thomaskirche anzunehmen, wobei ihr eine Wiederaufführung der Weimarer Kantate „Christen, ätzet diesen Tag" (BWV 63) vorangegangen sein muß. Noch nicht abgerissen war in jenen Jahren die auf das alte Verfahren der Magnificat-Tropierung sowie auf vorreformatorisches Brauchtum zurückgehende Tradition, das Magnificat zur Weihnachtszeit mit intermittierenden Liedern zu versehen, den *„Rotulae"* oder später so genannten *„Laudes"*. Vorläufig gescheitert war offenbar ein Versuch des Leipziger Rates (1702), *„die zur Weihnacht Zeit üblichen so genanten Laudes mit dem Joseph lieber Joseph mein, und Kindlein wiegen"* aus dem Gottesdienst zu verbannen. Während die 1678 in der Bibliothek der Thomasschule nachweisbaren *„Laudes wie sie zur Weynachts Zeit zwischen denen Magnificat gesungen werden mit 6 Stimmen u. Instrumenten"* leider verlorengegangen sind – damit fehlt ein zentraler Beleg für das liturgische Formular des 17. Jahrhunderts –, liegt ein entsprechendes Material aus dem Besitz des Thomaskantors Johann Kuhnau (1660–1722) noch vor. Der um 1720 teilweise erneuerte, mit Textmarken von der Hand Kuhnaus versehene und für Aufführungen in verschiedenen Tonarten eingerichtete Stimmensatz einer vermeintlichen Weihnachtskantate Kuhnaus (Musikbibliothek der Stadt Leipzig, Sammlung Becker III.2.124), hat, da es sich um eben die vier Texte handelt, die auch Bach für die Einlagesätze des Es-Dur-Magnificats verwendete, offenbar als separates Material für die *„Laudes"* zu gelten.

Von hier aus stellt sich die Frage, ob Bach zeitweilig erwogen haben könnte, für die *„Laudes"* auf ein vorgefundenes älteres Material zurückzugreifen, ehe er sich dann doch

Neukomposition entschloß. Keineswegs ist dabei nur an eine Amtsvorgänger Johann Kuhnau, Johann Schelle oder Sebastian Knüpfer zu denken, da die für Bach maßgebliche Tradition – wie Arbeiten von Martin Geck (1961, 1965) und Albrecht Tunger (1978) aufgezeigt haben – offenbar zu wesentlichen Teilen in das letzte Viertel des 16. Jahrhunderts zurückreicht. Das 1603 von Erhard Bodenschatz in Leipzig veröffentlichte und zur Zeit Bachs in der Thomasschulbibliothek sicherlich vorhandene „Florilegium selectissimarum cantionum" endet bemerkenswerterweise mit sechsstimmigen Sätzen über „Vom Himmel hoch", „Freut euch und jubiliert", „Gloria in excelsis" sowie „Joseph, lieber Joseph mein" aus der Feder des Sethus Calvisius (1556–1615, Thomaskantor seit 1594), und ein Anklang des Bachschen „Freut euch und jubiliert" an den Satz des Calvisius ist nicht zu überhören. Der Annahme, die vier Einlagesätze könnten in der Leipziger Thomaskirche von jener – der Chorempore gegenüberliegenden – kleinen „Schwalbennest"-Empore oberhalb des Triumphbogens aus erklungen sein, hat die neuere Forschung mit dem Hinweis auf Besetzungsschwierigkeiten und Platzmangel widersprochen. Angesichts des Verlustes von Bachs Aufführungsstimmen läßt sich eine befriedigende Antwort nicht geben. Zu bedenken bleibt jedoch, daß auf der noch bis 1727 mehrfach instandgesetzten kleineren Orgel der genannten Ostempore „in hohen Festen geschlagen und musiciret" wurde, und daß auch für die separate Ausfertigung des erwähnten, von Kuhnau herrührenden Aufführungsmaterials – hier werden vier Singstimmen, zwei Trompeten, Pauken, Streicher und Basso continuo erfordert – ein besonderer Anlaß bestanden haben muß. In jedem Falle aber wäre eine getrennte Aufstellung nur für Aufführungen in der Thomaskirche in Betracht zu ziehen, da die Nikolaikirche vergleichbare räumliche Möglichkeiten nicht besaß.

Ob Bach die Es-Dur-Fassung seines Magnificats auch nach 1723 noch aufgeführt hat, entzieht sich unserer Kenntnis. Philipp Spittas Bach-Biographie (1880) erwähnt – gegenwärtig nicht nachweisbare – Abschriften fremder, wohl italienischer Magnificat-Kompositionen von der Hand Bachs (Partituren) bzw. seiner Frau Anna Magdalena (Stimmen). Zieht man eine zeitübliche Handschriftenverwechselung in Betracht, so läßt sich annehmen, daß jene Stimmenabschriften von der Hand des Thomasschülers Johann Andreas Kuhnau stammen und in den Zeitraum 1723–1725 zu verweisen sind. In eines dieser Werke (D-Dur) soll Bach sogar die erwähnten vier Einlagesätze übertragen haben, wenngleich in teilweise abweichender Plazierung.* Noch erhalten sind im Unterschied zu den vorgenannten Kopien zwei Bachsche Abschriften aus der späteren Leipziger Zeit: ein Magnificat in C von Antonio Caldara (um 1670–1736) für vier Singstimmen, vier Trompeten und Pauken, Streicher und Basso continuo, sowie eine anonyme Komposition in C (BWV Anh. 30) für acht Singstimmen, drei Trompeten und Pauken, Streicher und Basso continuo.

Aus dem Rückgriff auf fremde Magnificat-Kompositionen dürfte sich wenigstens teilweise die eigenartige Tatsache erklären, daß Bach sich erst gegen 1730 veranlaßt sah, sein eigenes Werk aus der Es-Dur-Fassung in die mittlerweile auch für ihn gebräuchlichere Tonart D-Dur überzuführen.

Nachtrag:
Einige der von Spitta gemeinten Stimmensätze besitzt die Deutsche Staatsbibliothek Berlin (Mus. ms. anon. 1534_1536; Schreiber: meist J. A. Kuhnau und C. G. Gerlach, um 1730; Provenienz: Neue Kirche Leipzig). In Mus. ms. anon. 1535

Die in diesem Zusammenhang von ihm angefertigte sorgfältig disponierte und übersichtliche Reinschriftpartitur mit ihren genauen Besetzungsangaben und vergleichsweise reichlichen Vortragsbezeichnungen könnte an einen auswärtigen Auftrag, an Dedikations- oder Verleihzwecke denken lassen, doch fehlen für eine derartige Annahme weitere Anhaltspunkte.

Wichtigstes Charakteristikum der Neufassung (BWV 243) ist der Verzicht auf die vier weihnachtlichen Einlagesätze. Ob dies für Leipzig zugleich das Ende der „Laudes"-Tradition signalisiert, bleibt ungewiß. Veränderungen des Instrumentariums ließen sich bei der Tiefertransposition des ganzen Werkes schon aus Umfangsgründen nicht vermeiden. So wurde in Satz 3 die obligate Oboe durch eine Oboe d'amore ersetzt, Querflöten traten in Satz 9 an die Stelle der ursprünglichen Blockflöten, in Satz 10 mußte die Bassetto-Stimme der hohen Streicher den Violoncelli übergeben werden und in Satz 8 wurde infolge unumgänglicher Hochoktavierungen die Mitwirkung der Viola in der obligaten Streicherstimme unmöglich. Der auf einer Naturtrompete nur unbefriedigend zu realisierende Cantus firmus (Magnificat-Weise, 9. Psalmton) im „Suscepit Israel" wurde den Oboen übertragen, den col sordino zu spielenden Violinen in Satz 6 wurden die Flöten zugeordnet und schließlich hatten die Flöten in den Tuttisätzen Nr. 1, 4, 7 und 12 zusätzlich mitzuwirken, indem sie vorhandene Stimmen teils verstärkten, teils solistisch übernahmen oder aber hinzukomponierte Passagen vortrugen. Einher gingen alle diese Maßnahmen mit Bachs Bestreben, Harmonik und Stimmführung zu glätten und die Rhythmik weiter zu differenzieren.

Im Musikleben hat sich die reifere D-Dur-Fassung von Bachs Magnificat seit langem gegenüber der herberen Es-Dur-Frühfassung durchgesetzt. Versuchen, auch jener zu ihrem Recht zu verhelfen, ist Erfolg nur beschieden, wenn die Beschaffung geeigneter Blechblasinstrumente gelingt. Unsere Partiturausgabe versucht einen Mittelweg im Blick auf die Praxis insofern einzuschlagen, als sie der D-Dur-Fassung die weihnachtlichen Einlagesätze der Erstfassung einen Halbton tiefer transponiert zuordnet. In Kauf genommen werden mußte dabei das Risiko, daß Bach selbst eine derartige Transposition möglicherweise mit Änderungen in Stimmführung und Instrumentation verknüpft hätte. Die Vervollständigung des nur fragmentarisch überlieferten, jedoch in umgearbeiteter Form als Duett „Ehre sei Gott in der Höhe" in der 1725 komponierten Weihnachtskantate BWV 110 enthaltenen „Virga Jesse" folgt einem Vorschlag von Alfred Dürr (1951).

Die Generalbaßaussetzung lehnt sich weitgehend an diejenige in der 1909 von Karl Straube besorgten Partitur (EP 29a) an, verzichtet jedoch auf deren Differenzierung zwischen Orgel und Cembalo. Ohnehin bieten die Quellen zu Bachs Magnificat nur eine schmale Beobachtungsbasis zur Klärung von Fragen wie Doppelakkompagnement oder Beschränkung der Orgelbegleitung auf die Chorsätze. Daß Bach in der D-Dur-Fassung das Continuosystem von Satz 6 ursprünglich wohl als Organo zu bezeichnen beabsichtigte, dann aber Cont: vorschrieb, sei immerhin nicht verschwiegen.

Hans-Joachim Schulze

(Magnificat D-Dur) befinden sich drei ältere Stimmen (um 1720) aus dem Besitz des Thomaskantors Johann Kuhnau; nachträgliche Hinweise auf die vier Einlagesätze sind teilweise von J. Kuhnau geschrieben und zielen offenbar auf die oben erwähnte Quelle MB Leipzig Slg. Becker III. 2. 124

CONCLUDING REMARKS

As one of the Cantica maiora of the Roman Catholic Office, Mary's hymn of praise, the Magnificat (Canticum Beatae Mariae Virginis), has long occupied a special position in the liturgy and, at least since the 6th century, has formed the climax of the vesper service. With the dawn of the Age of Netherlands Polyphony in the 15th century the traditional psalmodic rendition of the New Testament text (Luke 1 : 46–55) was joined by a tradition of motet settings whose extensive literature, produced over the next 200 years, was enriched by nearly all of the more important composers from Dunstable and Dufay to Morales, Lasso, Palestrina and Johann Walter.

From about 1600 on the text of the Magnificat, along with the Requiem and the Te Deum, was particularly favored by composers for elaborate, concertante settings. The number of such compositions is incalculable. One need only think of Monteverdi, Schütz, and Buxtehude in the 17th century, and Albinoni, the Bach sons Carl Philipp Emanuel and Johann Christian, Caldara, Galuppi, Graupner, Harrer, W. A. Mozart, Sammartini, Telemann, Vivaldi, and Zelenka in the 18th century. Although the Magnificat text fell out of favor during the 19th century (apart from Mendelssohn's there is hardly any setting from the period worthy of mention), it has attracted interest again in recent times—as the significant settings of Ernst Pepping and Krzystof Penderecki, among others, attest.

The crowning achievement of this extensive tradition is, without question, the Magnificat of Johann Sebastian Bach, a work which, by virtue of its orchestral brilliance, its compositional concentration and intensity, the variety of its constituent movements and its profundity of textual exegesis, far transcends all previously established norms. It is not clear whether this work, Bach's only known setting of the Magnificat (one that survives in two versions: E-flat and D major), was in fact his only contribution to the genre. His estate is said to have included *"numerous Oratorios, Masses, Magnificat, independent Sanctus settings . . ."* The so-called "small Magnificat", long considered lost, turned out, upon its rediscovery, to be a church cantata dating from around 1708; its autograph, a composing score, suggests that the composer was Georg Philipp Telemann. The question, however, has not yet been completely resolved.

Bach apparently composed the E-flat version of the Magnificat in December, 1723. It is his first large-scale vocal work in Leipzig. The *tempus clausum*, the four-week silent period lasting from the first through the fourth Sundays of Advent, during which no concerted music was performed in the Leipzig service, apparently afforded Bach his first opportunity after his having assumed the Thomas Cantorate to prepare a composition of these proportions—one that contains entirely newly composed music throughout. The hasty handwriting and the large number of corrections in the autograph score are, accordingly, not to be understood as symptomatic, perhaps, of a lack of time, but, on the contrary, as evidence of the extraordinary care with which Bach prepared this work.

There are a number of indications, moreover, that the Magnificat presented Bach with a new compositional situation. There was, for example, initial uncertainty about the scoring of the chorus. After having begun to write for four voices, Bach decided on a five-part chorus consisting of Soprano, Alto I and II, Tenor and Bass. Only later did he arrive at the present division of the sopranos into Soprano I and II. The choice of the key of E-flat for a work with trumpets and timpani is both unique and puzzling. It may reflect Bach's desire to avoid this time his previously exclusive choice of the key of C major for works featuring these instruments. He was not to employ the key that ultimately was to be his preferred tonality for this scoring, D major, until New Year's, 1724. An alternative (and less convincing) explanation for the E-flat tonality of the first version is that Bach had planned in this case to make use of a procedure that he had previously only resorted to as a necessary expedient: namely, employing woodwinds tuned in "tief Kammerton" (low chamber pitch), and accordingly tuning the strings down a half-step. The result (notated E-flat = sounding D) would have made the use of the D trumpet possible. Further evidence, finally, of Bach's lack of familiarity with certain Leipzig practices at this time is the fact that he inserted the four additional movements based on Christmas texts into the work after it had been completed—an action that had undesirable consequences for the tonal organization of the whole. Since Bach, during his first year of service in Leipzig had felt constrained to jot down, as a precaution, the complicated liturgy of the First Sunday of Advent in a cantata score, and since he had even described himself as late as April, 1724, during the course of a controversy, as a *"stranger, unfamiliar with the customs here"*, it does not seem unreasonable to see in the E-flat Magnificat the product of a stage of searching, testing and experimenting.

The vesper service of the two principal Leipzig churches St. Nicholas and St. Thomas, provided that the Magnificat was to be *"sung in German on regular Sundays but performed [musiciret] in Latin on high feasts."* (Chr. E. Sicul, *Annales Lipsienses*, Leipzig, 1717). The *"high feasts"* in this instance were the first and second days of Christmas, Easter and Pentecost. But the opportunity for *"musical"*, i. e., concerted performances of the Magnificat arose on other holidays as well, such as Ascension or the Marian feasts.

Since it was usual to perform the *"main work"* [*Hauptmusik*], i. e., the cantata, on the first day of a major feast in the morning service of the Nikolaikirche and to repeat it in the Thomaskirche during vespers (the order on the second day was reversed), we may assume that the first performance of the E-flat version of the Magnificat took place on the afternoon of 25 December 1723 in the Thomaskirche, where it must have followed a reperformance of the Weimar cantata *"Christen, ätzet diesen Tag"* (BWV 63).

At this time the old custom had not yet been abandoned of troping the Magnificat text during the Christmas season with interpolated hymns known as *"Rotulae"* or, later, *"Laudes"*. This tradition dated back to the pre-Reformation period. In 1702 the Leipzig council had attempted, without success, to ban the *"so-called Laudes Joseph lieber Joseph mein an Kindlein wiegen"* from the Christmas service. A collection of *"Laudes for 6 Voices and Instruments, as sung during the Christmas season with the Magnificat"*, a collection known to have been in the library of the Thomasschule in 1678, is no longer extant. Its loss deprives us of a central source for Leipzig liturgical practice in the 17th century. But other material of a related nature, once in the possession of the Thomaskantor Johann Kuhnau (1660–1722) does survive. It is a set of performing parts now preserved in the Musikbibliothek der Stadt Leipzig (Becker Sammlung III.2.124). The set was partially revised around the year 1720 by Kuhnau himself for performance in various keys and contains text cues in his hand. The parts have been thought to be for a Christmas cantata. But since precisely the same four tex-

are involved as were used by Bach for the interpolated movements of the E-flat Magnificat, Kuhnau's manuscript must evidently be considered as comprising separate material for the *"Laudes"*.

At this point the question arises whether Bach, before having decided to compose the *"Laudes"* anew, could ever have contemplated using older, pre-existent material for them. If so, he would not have been limited just to the works of his predecessors Johann Kuhnau, Johann Schelle or Sebastian Knüpfer. Recent studies by Martin Geck (1961, 1965) and Albrecht Tunger (1978) have demonstrated that a substantial part of this tradition, insofar as it pertains to Bach, extended as far back as the last quarter of the 16th century. The *"Florilegium selectissimarum cantionum"*, published by Erhard Bodenschatz in Leipzig in 1603 and undoubtedly still available in the library of the Thomasschule in Bach's time, concludes, remarkably enough, with *"Vom Himmel hoch"*, *"Freut euch und jubiliert"*, *"Gloria in excelsis"* and *"Joseph, lieber Joseph mein"* in six-part settings composed by Sethus Calvisius (1556–1615, Thomaskantor since 1594). There is, furthermore, an unmistakable similarity between Bach's setting of *"Freut euch und jubiliert"* and that of Calvisius.

It has been suggested that the four interpolated movements could have sounded in the Thomaskirche from a small "swallow's nest", located above the triumphal arch and facing the choir loft. Recent research, however, had rejected this assumption, pointing to the lack of room as well as of orchestral players. Since Bach's performing parts are lost, no satisfactory answer to this question can be advanced. But it is worth noting that the small organ located in the East loft just mentioned was repaired frequently until 1727 and was *played and performed upon on high feasts*". Moreover, there must also have been a special occasion that prompted Kuhnau to prepare the separate set of parts (consisting of four voices, two trumpets, timpani, strings and continuo) discussed above. In any case, a performance with separated forces could only have taken place in the Thomaskirche; for the Nikolaikirche did not possess comparable spatial resources.

We do not know whether Bach ever performed the E-flat version of the Magnificat again after 1723. Philipp Spitta's Bach biography (1880) mentions Magnificat settings by other (presumably Italian) composers that were copied in both Bach's hand (scores) and in that of his wife Anna Magdalena (parts). This can no longer be verified. One may assume, though, allowing for a handwriting confusion common in Spitta's day, that the parts were actually copied between 1723 and 1725 by Johann Andreas Kuhnau, a pupil at the Thomasschule. It is also claimed that Bach transferred the four interpolated movements to one of these works, a composition in D major, although he did not place them in exactly the same positions they occupy in the E-flat Magnificat.* In contrast to the lost copies mentioned by Spitta, two copies in Bach's handwriting and dating from the later Leipzig period do survive: a Magnificat in C by Antonio Caldara (c. 1670–1736) for four voices, four trumpets, timpani, strings and continuo, and an anonymous setting in C (BWV Anh. 30) for eight voices, three trumpets, timpani, strings and continuo.

Bach's having resorted to the Magnificat settings of other composers helps explain, to some degree at least, the remarkable fact that it was not until around 1730 that he had any need to recast his own composition into what had in the meantime become for him the more normal key of D major. The carefully planned layout and unusual legibility of the fair copy score that Bach prepared on this occasion, along with its precise instructions regarding the scoring and the relatively complete performance indications, raise the question whether the score may have been written for an outside commission, or as a dedication copy, or as a manuscript to be loaned out. There is, however, no other evidence for speculation along these lines.

The most important feature of the new version (BWV 243) is the absence of the four Christmas numbers. It is not clear whether their removal attests to the end of the Leipzig "Laudes" tradition. The changes in instrumental ranges resulting from the transposition of the work inevitably led to changes in instrumentation. In Movement 3 the obbligato oboe was replaced by an oboe d'amore; in Movement 9 transverse flutes replaced the recorders of the first version; in Movement 10 the bassetto part for the upper strings had to be ceded to the violoncello; and unavoidable octave transpositions in Movement 8 led to the elimination of the viola from the obbligato string part. In the *"Suscepit Israel"* movement the cantus firmus (= the plainsong Magnificat melody in the 9th psalm tone) was now assigned to the oboe, its rendition on a natural trumpet presumably having proven to be unsatisfactory. The "col sordino" violin part in Movement 6 was transferred to the flutes. Finally, flutes were added in the tutti movements 1, 4, 7, and 12. Their parts were either newly composed or derived from pre-existing lines which were now either reinforced or simply newly assigned to the flutes. Along with all these changes there are autograph corrections reflecting Bach's concerns with smoothness of the harmonic progressions and the voice leading and his interest in increasing the degree of rhythmic differentiation.

The more mature D-major version of the Magnificat has long since eclipsed the more austere E-flat version in our musical life. But attempts to do full justice to the latter succeed only when the appropriate brass instruments are obtained. In practical terms the present edition of the score attempts to follow a middle course by transposing the Christmas interpolations of the first version and including them in the D-major version—this despite the risk that Bach himself in such a situation might have combined the transposition with changes of voice leading and instrumentation. The fragmentary movement "Virga Jesse" exists, in a different form, as the duet *"Ehre sei Gott in der Höhe"* in the Christmas cantata BWV 110, composed in 1725. The reconstruction offered here follows a suggestion of Alfred Dürr (1951).

The continuo realization makes extensive use of the one provided by Karl Straube in his 1909 edition of the score (EP 29a) but does not observe his differentiation between organ and harpsichord. The sources for Bach's Magnificat provide in any case very little evidence bearing on the question of double accompaniment or the restriction of the organ to the choral movements. May it not go unmentioned, however, that Bach apparently intended at first to label the continuo line in Movement 6 of the D-major version *Organo* but then wrote down *Cont:* instead.

Hans-Joachim Schulze

---

* Cf. addenda p. 77